Y0-BDQ-026

THEY TELL IT LIKE IT IS

Chuck Berry . . . Phil Spector . . . Frank Zappa . . . Tim Hardin . . . James Brown . . . Elvis Presley . . . Tim Buckley . . . The Doors . . . Brian Wilson . . . Otis Redding . . . the other masters of the new sound. . . .

Their lyrics are not the kind Tin Pan Alley used to grind out—or the sort found in poetry textbooks. They are of the here and now, filled with the objects and emotions of life as it is lived today, mirroring the hopes, fears, and yearnings of an intense and restless generation.

If you want to know what it's like to be young in America in the second half of the twentieth century, look for the truth and nothing but the truth in—

ROCK IS BEAUTIFUL

ROCK IS BEAUTIFUL

An Anthology of American Lyrics, 1953–1968

EDITED BY
STEPHANIE SPINNER

INTRODUCTION BY
NAT HENTOFF

A DELL BOOK

Published by
Dell Publishing Co., Inc.
750 Third Avenue
New York, N.Y. 10017
Copyright © 1970 by Stephanie Spinner
Introduction © 1970 by Dell Publishing Co., Inc.
All rights reserved. No part of this book
may be reproduced in any form or by any means
without the prior written permission of the Publisher,
excepting brief quotes used in connection with reviews
written specifically for inclusion in a magazine or newspaper.
Dell ® TM 681510, Dell Publishing Co., Inc.
Printed in the United States of America
First printing—February 1970

This book is dedicated to
THE VETERANS OF THE FIFTIES.

ACKNOWLEDGMENTS

Thanks to: Steve Berke, Steve Berns, Elizabeth Capelle, Clark Dimond, Edward Konick, Carol Krueger, Peter Locke, Megan Parry, Ira Rosen, and *Hit Parader* magazine.

INTRODUCTION

One young member of the English department at a Brooklyn high school, has instituted a course he calls "The Modern Ballad." "Actually," he tells me, "our texts are rock lyrics. But with that title, the venture appears more respectable." Increasingly, at other schools, the songs of rock are entering the curriculum—often without any disguise at all. I much prefer the latter approach. Rock is its own open-ended category. Why try to constrict it with traditional "educational" tags?

Similarly, there is no reason to limit rock lyrics to English courses. In its natural habitat—at home, in jukeboxes, at dances, in the global village that is the transistor radio—rock asks, and sometimes tries to answer, all manner of questions. And it reflects a broad spectrum of attitudes, yearnings, fulfillments, fantasies. Rock can be personal or collective, apolitical or polemical. It can be banal or piercingly evocative.

And rock is also history—social history, aural history. Looking through Stephanie Spinner's anthology—hearing as you read—is like looking at a kaleidoscope of what a particular generation of the young has felt about its country. To some it is an alien, hostile land—but they know no other. Others want to change it. And there are those who stake out a groove in it for themselves, finding the further frontier inside their heads.

I know it is modish to speak of the lyrics of rock as "poetry." And there is some poetry here—quixotic, picaresque, careeningly or reflectively lyrical. But there are other songs here no more poetic than the *Congressional Record,* yet they belong in this anthology too. For Stephanie Spinner has encompassed the whole rock experience—and the experience of being young in this America that is at the root of rock.

Home, for instance—home is love because it's home;

but it's also status-symbol land, and in "So Long, Dad," it's beyond wanting to reclaim. How you feel about it depends on where you've been and where you're at.

School is the clock or just another set of orders, or a community (outside class), or the last chance before limbo. Depends on where you've been and where you're at.

But rock itself may take you out of school while you're sitting there. A writer for *The Fifth Estate*, telling of a concert by Big Brother and the Holding Company: "They play because they dig it. They play the way they feel it. It's probably the secret dream of every kid everywhere to just do things they dig doing and be rewarded for it. America, as only America, the land where dreams come true, could, is making that dream come true for Big Brother." Please buy my record, says Johnny B. Goode. You can become an all-American boy by buying a guitar and then maybe you'll get with those Nashville cats who play clean as country water and *you'll* be a rock and roll star.

"And rock is also educational," says Frank Zappa. "How to ask a girl for a date, what love is like." Whether you ever get with those Nashville cats or not. Do you wanna dance? And after? Rock can't tell you that; it just sounds the options.

Rock, furthermore, can be a sense of place as well as of options. On Broadway—or much more privately, up on the roof or under the boardwalk. It's the balm of California (forgetting about the freeways) or summer in the city. Which city? More to the point is which part of which city. Discover glorious Harlem in New York City.

And there are times when a sense of place has no bottom—when you're the family's unowned boy, as Tim Hardin would put it. Lonely in a cell, a literal cell or a room at heartbreak hotel. But there's always that other American dream—the road. Mobility may not be all, but it can do for a man of means, by no means king of the road. And you never know whom you'll meet and get turned around by, like the lady who came from Baltimore.

Rock speaks too of the machines that bring the power of mobility. For country blues singers it was the railroad train. But in the time of rock, it's black denim trousers and motorcycle boots, fast cars, old cars, moving in style. But if you have a little modified pon-ton, you can be the coolest thing around and ride through that landscape with style.

Style is also attitude—Charlie Brown walking into the classroom cool and slow. And style may dislodge fantasy. He sure ain't the boy I been dreaming of/But he's sure the boy I love. But is love enough? Depends on where you've been and where you're at. Parents can separate you from the leader of the pack or from someone who's black. Like Frank Zappa says, rock is educational—but only up to a point.

Then there's inner space, varieties of highs and downs. Are you really floating, just relaxed and paying attention, or are you in a psychedelic dungeon? Not everybody's in every song. Not every girl either, but nearly all kinds are in one or another. Hot rod queens, rare roses in Spanish Harlem, and of course, supergirls—depending on your fantasy.

But moving out of the circle of self and the circle of two, there is still this country. The times may be a-changin', but the perspective shifts and overturns, again depending on where you are—deep in the heart of Harlem, or totin' a gun while not believing in war, or counting the cars on the New Jersey turnpike. As the beat goes on, James Brown turns into Horatio Alger but then becomes black and proud (we'd rather die on our feet than keep living on our knees). And Van Dyke Parks observes from a distance, microscopically. Contradictions? Well, they've all come to look for America, and they're still finding out.

And beyond, beyond the end of being young? Get a job; blue Monday; money, honey, if you want to get along with me. Poverty train for some and for others, squandering your life with bigger cars and bigger houses? But there are other ways. Which ways? Rock can't tell you that. Rock can tell you, as Bob Dylan says, that "Lifelessness is the Great Enemy & always wears a hip guard—he is very hip-guard." But what does that *mean?*

Well, it's not so much meaning as being. And rock is where a generation has been. They're going to go all kinds of ways, some with and some without hip guards. But all of them have been here, in the lyrics here.

New York, March 1969 —NAT HENTOFF

CONTENTS

PART ONE

PART TWO

PART ONE

It's been a long time coming
But I know a change is gonna come

—SAM COOKE

Jimmy Radcliffe/Carl Spencer

Deep in the Heart of Harlem

A dog barkin' at the crack of dawn
A woman cryin' 'cause her man is gone
I toss and turn and then I stretch and yawn
Another morning, another day
Deep in the heart of Harlem
I feel the tenement comin' alive
Another working day I've got to survive
Fight with the foreman from eight thirty to five
To make a dollar so I can live
Deep in the heart of Harlem
I push and kick and get my feelings hurt
Downtown I'm just a little spoke
That helps the wheel go round
If I was right maybe I'd move away
Out to the country where my kids could play
But I can't make it on my poor man's pay
We got to stay here, can't get away
Deep in the heart of Harlem.

© 1963 January Music Corporation, a subsidiary of A. Schroeder Music Corporation. All rights reserved. International copyright secured.

Jerry Leiber/Cynthia Weil/Mike Stoller/ Barry Mann

Only in America

Only in America
Can a guy from anywhere
Go to sleep a pauper
And wake up a millionaire
Only in America
Can a kid without a cent
Get a break and maybe grow
Up to be President

Only in America
Can a kid who's washing cars
Take a giant step and reach right up
And touch the stars
Only in America
Could a dream like this come true
Could a boy like me start with
Nothing and end up with you
Only in America
Land of opportunity
Would a classy girl like you
Fall for a poor boy like me.

© Copyright 1963 by Screen Gems–Columbia Music, Inc., New York, N.Y. Used by permission. Reproduction prohibited.

Sam Cooke

A Change Is Gonna Come

I was born by the river
In a little old tent
And just like the river
I've been running ever since
It's been a long time coming
But I know a change is gonna come

It's been too hard living
And I'm afraid to die
I don't know what's up there
Beyond the sky
It's been a long time coming
But I know a change is gonna come

There's the time I went to my brother
I asked my brother "Will you help me, please?"
He turned me down and then I asked my mother
I said "Mother, I'm down on my knees . . ."

Every time I fall I know
It won't last too long
And somehow right now
I feel I'm able to carry on
It's been a long time coming
But I know a change is gonna come.

© Copyright 1964 by Kags Music Corp.

P. F. Sloan

Eve of Destruction

The eastern world, it is explodin'
Violence flarin' and bullets loadin'
You're old enough to kill, but not for votin'
You don't believe in war,
But what's that gun you're totin'?
And even the Jordan River
Has bodies floatin'
But you tell me
Over and over and over again, my friend
You don't believe we're on the eve of destruction
Don't you understand what I'm trying to say?
Can't you see the fear that I'm feelin' today?
If the button is pushed there's no running away
There'll be no one to save with the world in a grave
Take a look around you, boy
It's bound to scare you, boy
But you tell me
Over and over and over again, my friend
You don't believe we're on the eve of destruction
My blood's so mad, feels like coagulatin'
I'm sittin' here, just contemplatin'
You can't twist the truth, it knows no regulation
And a handful of senators don't pass legislation
Marches alone can't bring integratin'
When human respect is disintegratin'
This whole crazy world is just too frustratin'
And you tell me
Over and over and over again, my friend
That you don't believe we're on the eve of destruction
Think of all the hate there is in Red China

© 1965 Trousdale Music Publishers, Inc., 1330 Avenue of the Americas, New York, N.Y. 10019. All rights reserved. Used by permission.

Then take a look around Selma, Alabama
You may leave here for four days in space
But when you return it's the same old place
The pounding of the drums, and pride, and disgrace
You can bury your dead but don't leave a trace
Hate your next-door neighbor
But don't forget to say grace
And you tell me
Over and over and over again, my friend
That you don't believe we're on the eve of destruction.

Loretta Lynn

Dear Uncle Sam

Dear Uncle Sam, I know you're a busy man
And tonight I write to you through tears with a tremblin'
hand
My darling answered when he got that call from you
You said you really need him, but you don't need him like
I do.

Don't misunderstand I know he's fighting for our land
I really love my country, but I also love my man
He proudly wears the colors of the old red, white, and
blue
While I wear a heartache since he left me for you.

Dear Uncle Sam, I just got your telegram
And I can't believe that this is me shakin' like I am
For it said "I'm sorry to inform you. . . ."

© Copyright 1965 by Sure-Fire Music Co., Inc. Used by permission.

Janis Ian

Society's Child

Come to my door, baby
Face is clean and shining black as night
My mother went to answer, you know
That you look so fine
Now I could understand your tears and your shame
She called you boy instead of your name
When she wouldn't let you inside
When she turned and said
But honey, he's not our kind
She says I can't see you anymore, baby
Can't see you anymore
No, I don't want to see you anymore, baby.

Walk me down to school, baby
Everybody's acting deaf and blind
Until they turn and say
Why don't you stick to your own kind
My teachers all laugh, their smirking stares cutting deep
down in our affairs
Preachers of equality think they believe it
Then why won't they just let us be
They say I can't see you anymore, baby
Can't see you anymore
No, I don't want to see you anymore, baby.

One of these days I'm gonna stop my listening
Gonna raise my head up high
One of these days I'm gonna raise up my glistening wings
and fly
But that day will have to wait for awhile
Baby, I'm only society's child
When we're older things may change
But for now this is the way they must remain

© Copyright 1966 by Dialogue Music, Inc. Used by permission.

I say I can't see you anymore, baby
Can't see you anymore
No, I don't want to see you anymore, baby.

Stephen Stills

For What It's Worth

There's something happening here
What it is ain't exactly clear
There's a man with a gun over there
Tellin' me I've got to beware
I think it's time we stop, children,
What's that sound?
Everybody look what's goin' down.

There's battle lines bein' drawn
Nobody's right if everybody's wrong
Young people speakin' their minds
Gettin' so much resistance from behind
I think it's time we stop, children,
What's that sound?
Everybody look what's goin' down.

What a field day for the heat
A thousand people in the street
Singin' songs and carryin' signs
Mostly say "Hooray for our side"
I think it's time we stop, children,
What's that sound?
Everybody look what's goin' down.

Paranoia strikes deep
Into your life it will creep
It starts when you're always afraid
Step out of line, the man come and take you away
I think it's time we stop, children,
What's that sound?
Everybody look what's goin' down.

Copyright © 1966, 1967 by Ten-East Music, Cotillion Music, Inc., and Springalo Toones.

Sonny Bono

The Beat Goes On

The beat goes on
The beat goes on
Drums keep pounding rhythm to the brain
Lad-i-da-de-de
Lad-i-da-de-di.

Charleston was once the rage uh ha
History has turned a page uh ha
The mini skirt is the current thing uh ha
Teeny bopper is our new born king uh ha
And the beat goes on
The beat goes on
Drums keep pounding rhythm to the brain
Lad-i-da-de-de
Lad-i-da-de-di.

The grocery store's a supermart uh ha
Little girls will break their hearts uh ha
And men still keep on marching off to war
Electrically they keep a baseball score
And the beat goes on
The beat goes on
Drums keep pounding rhythm to the brain
Lad-i-da-de-de
Lad-i-da-de-di.

Grandmas sit in chairs and reminisce
Boys keep chasing girls to get a kiss
The cars keep a-goin' faster all the time
Bums still cry "hey, buddy have you got a dime"
And the beat goes on

Copyright © 1967 by Cotillion Music, Inc., and Chris Marc Music, Inc., 1841 Broadway, New York, N.Y. 10023.

The beat goes on
Drums keep pounding rhythm to the brain
Lad-i-da-de-de
Lad-i-da-de-di
And the beat goes on
Yes the beat goes on
And the beat goes on
The beat goes on.

The Unknown Soldier

Wait until the war is over
And we're both a little older
The unknown soldier
Practice where the news is read
Television children dead
Unborn living, living dead
Bullet strikes the helmet's head
And—it's all over for the unknown soldier,
It's all over for the unknown soldier, oh yeah . . .
("Company halt!" "Present arms!")
Make a grave for the unknown soldier
Nestled in your hollow shoulder
The unknown soldier
Practice where the news is read
Television children dead
Bullet strikes the helmet's head
It's all over—
The war is over,
The war is over.

Copyright © 1968 by Nipper Music Company, Inc. All rights reserved.

Tim Buckley

No Man Can Find the War

Photographs of guns and flame
Scarlet skull and distant game
Bayonet and jungle grin
Nightmares dreamed by bleeding men
Lookouts tremble on the shore
But no man can find the war.

Tape recorders echo scream
Orders fly like bullet stream
Drums and cannon laugh aloud
Whistles come from ashen shroud
Leaders damn the world and roar
But no man can find the war.

Is the war across the sea?
Is the war behind the sky?
Have you each and all gone blind?
Is the war inside your mind?

Humans weep at human death
All the talkers lose their breath
Movies paint a chaos tale
Singers see and poets wail
All the world knows the score
But no man can find the war.

© 1967 by Third Story Music.

Peter Rowan

Home of the Brave

It took us so long to get home
And I've been down so long
People all around me
They can't understand
How I lost my hand
But the war was grand
A lovely parade

Here is where I long to be
My home the grave, my land is free
And I know it's paid for
Yes very well paid for
And I know it's paid for
Yes very well paid for

It took us so long to get home
And you bring me so far down
People gather round me
Try to understand
About my hand
But the war was grand
A lovely parade.

Copyright © 1968 Nina Music. All rights reserved.

Randy Newman

The Beehive State

Since you're the delegate from Kansas
Will you kindly take the floor
And tell us what is Kansas thinking?
And what is Kansas for?
Well, Kansas is for the farmer
We stand behind the little man
And we need
So help us if you can.
I see the gentleman from Utah
Our friendly Beehive State
How can we help you, Utah?
How can we make you great?
Well, we got to irrigate our desert
We got to get some things to grow
We got to tell this country about Utah—
Because nobody seems to know.

© 1968 January Music Corporation, a subsidiary of A. Schroeder Music Corporation. All rights reserved. International copyright secured.

James Brown/Hayward E. Moore

America Is My Home, Part 1

Ha ha
Talkin' 'bout me leavin' America
You got to be crazy
Man, I like all the nice things, Jack
Continental suits and things
Look-a-here
Now I'm sorry for the man
Who don't love this land
Now black and white they may fight
But if the enemy come we'll get together
And run him out of sight
Now look-a-here
The sun don't come out in rainy weather
But when you boil it down they're still together
Now let's not overlook the fact that we're, we're still in
reach
You got a chance to make it
And you got freedom of speech
Say what you wanna
Tell 'em how you feel
There may be a lot of places, a lot of places that you'd like
to go
But believe me, if you get an education you can't blow it,
you can't hardly blow it.

Now dig this
Now you tell me if I'm wrong
America is still the best country and that's without a doubt
America is still the best country without a doubt
And if anybody says it ain't
You just try to put 'em out

© Copyright 1968 Dynatone Publishing Co. Reprinted by permission of the publisher.

They ain't going nowhere
You got a good fight.

When I told you one time that I was a shoeshine boy
Every word I said I meant
But name me any other country you can start as a shoeshine boy and shake hands with the President
It ain't gonna happen
You got to have that royal blood to make it
And I ain't got nothing royal but me
So, I can't take the chances
I'm gonna stay home
And look-a-here
I got a brand new jet when I need to move
A soul brother made it now ain't that a groove
So look-a-here
Brothers and sisters and friends dig this
So quit your dreaming all night
Stop pitying yourself and get up and fight
Don't give out, you might give up
But just don't give out
I tell you if you give out don't give up
Just don't quit going
I mean like keep it movin' you know
'Cause if you stop like the ball'll quit rollin'
Now we got tours that carry us from Florida to Rome
But you know there's one thing we'll never forget
America's still our home
Hit it band
God bless America
I'm talking about me, too, you know
I'm American myself and I like that kind of thing.

Van Dyke Parks

Song Cycle

Palm Desert

By Palm Desert to market to buy. Tenderfoot up to date palms of the real estate. By Palm Desert springs often run dry.

I came west unto Hollywood, never-never land. Juxtaposed to B.B.D. and O. Beyond San Fernando on hillside manors on the banks of toxicity those below and those above the same.

Dreams are still born in Hollywood I don't understand. Just suppose the youngster knows he's had a good deal of fortune and up through the babble on the fair banks complicity, buy your leave or stay beyond the game.

Palm Desert not fade away. Palm Desert I wish I could stay. Palm Desert sages abound. So head your head to the ground round.

Meanwhile in the wild west of Hollywood age is losing hold. Inasmuch as you are touched to have withstood by the very old search for the truth within the bounds of toxicity. Left unsung so I have strung the frame.

Widows Walk

Widows walk ado walk on as in years of yore. The thought of you divided thus! It just may be due to discuss in cold turkey mourning in the willows. Or was it the wind. You recollect we all suspect the mortal door will open the sore

© 1968 by Found Farms Ballads, used by permission of Van Dyke Parks.

mind. The widows walk and wail among the willows. Widows walk ado walk on.

Widows face the future. Factories face the poor. The fact remains the peril strains the mind a bit. To have done and quit with it widows walk and wail among the willows. Widows walk ado walk on.

I'm guessing this is called civil, regrettably strife. So lessen your appalled pall mall and middle life. Long last a hymn to Him to help you on your way.

Contented is the boat. By chance how forlorn the shore. I've meant to take the chance to turn you 'bout the floor so trim the prim the lame have rose to say widows walk and wail among the willows. Widows walk and do is do the willows. Widows walk ado walk on.

Laurel Canyon Blvd.

What's up Laurel Canyon, hay. What is up in Laurel Canyon the seat of the beat to greet and eat at the heart of their companion way. That's up Laurel Canyon. And what is up the canyon will even eventually come down.

Tracks of the beaten in automobile pound the from-nine-to-fivers round a long line of drivers wind to dine in the divers and dandy line. One line bled in tandom from some new hatchet deals.

Cracks in the heat and then caught by the wheel catch the country store feel for the hackamore crew view the crackerbare coterie standing by. One line bred randyrand and too few wretched meals.

The All Golden

He is not your run-of-the-mill garden variety Alabama country fair. Left on Silver Lake he keeps a small apartment 'top an Oriental food store there. He returned to Alabama to see what he could see.

Off the record he is hungry though he works hard in his Alabama country fair. I should think he'd fade away the way that Bohemians often bare the frigid air. He returned from Alabama to see what he could see.

Constant commentary by the wayside. Nowadays them country boys don't cotton much to one two three four. Rest your team. Work out in the All Golden! You will know why hayseeds go back to the country.

Constant calm might still our stately union. Nowadays a Yankee dread not take his time to wend to sea. Forget to bear your arms in the All Golden. You will know why hayseeds go back to the country.

Might as well not 'low for one more go round. That's all folks. Them hayseeds go back to the country. Ja git it? Alright.

Van Dyke Parks

Yet all my dreams shall be nearer my God to Thee. Nearer my God to Thee. Nearer to Thee.

Public Domain

Our lowly liquor lobby longs to back a road to old time songs. Biblebelts worn from here and after all were born in the know.

So rally round awhile Jim Crow for I thought I'd like to show they can recall the Alamo way down in old Mexico.

Academia

I left Academia amid sixty-two. Was it sixty-one scholar was cooled from the U. Doubtless more on sore wing than prayer I up and just withdrew to the wander round there.

The Attic

I was there upon a four poster there. Mind touseled I came to bear some thoughts from the past amid a dash of influenza. And then I came to see in baggage the memories of truncated souvenirs. The war years. High moon I said high moon lighted high moon eye to my moon.

Far beyond the blue mist enveloped lawn the blanketed night comes on. The champagne is dead and gone. The forest around sensitive sound forest primeval. Through the panes cloud buttermilk war remains and twisted cross war refrains lunatic so high moon I said high moon lighted high moon eye to my moon.

Your age will most probably carry away the letters enveloped in carrion. Vague unpleasantries of the war. May your son's progenitorship of the state haphazardly help him to carry on. God send your son safe home to you. High Moon. You're eye to my moon.

By the People

Strike up the band brother hand me another bowl of your soul. Brother has a long way to go maybe baby should know his cotton mouth is too slow for the song of the forgotten South, just don't hang us up here.

Step by step by please though proletarian am I. By chance am you gwine git out de way o' de darkies. You'd better hustle up a storm to sing this Caucasian lullaby. Sleep oh my darling now sleep.

Draw freehand over Iron Curtain. Stalk up on the trim bamboo. To footridge the bullrushes certain to know law, American express. No Caucasian flair for flim-flam will do. Step by please step by.

Weigh the small advance. There is still a chance. Let's assume that we form a company men. No mention should then pass in revue of the show. Just understand that I prefer to be dead than red white or blue as I write sturdy crew. As you view these few Russians whose true dawn came to view long ago. So I think that you'd better strike up the band brother hand me another bowl of your soul. The song of the forgotten South just don't hang us up here. Here the unknown is at hand and not far from my heel a tarbaby feel for the Czar. For those who are lonely well the Black Sea is callin' Georgia's Stalin has fallen so you all come here. We now are near to the end. If you stay with the show say we all had to go to hasten to jar the few nations too far gone to step by.

Pot Pourri

A Southwester in the yard invested with the garden and camped in concentrattion of a tall lilac to peel the rust off purple arbor. Time is not the main thought from under the rain wrought from roots that brought us coots to hoot and haul us all back to the prime ordeal. Dust off Pearl Harbor time.

James Brown

Say It Loud—I'm Black and I'm Proud

Say it loud, I'm black and I'm proud
Say it loud, I'm black and I'm proud
Some people say we got a lot of malice
Some say it's a lot of nerve
But I say we won't quit moving
Until we get what we deserve
We've been 'buked and we've been scorned
We've been treated bad, talked about as sure as you're born
But just as sure as it takes two eyes to make a pair
Brother we can't quit until we get our share.

Whoee—out of sight tomorrow night—it's tough
You're tough enough—whoee—it's hurting me
Say it loud, I'm black and I'm proud
Say it loud, I'm black and I'm proud
Say it loud, I'm black and I'm proud.

I've worked on jobs with my feet and my hands
But all that work I did was for the other man
Now we demand a chance to do things for ourselves
We're tired of beating our head against the wall
And working for someone else
We're people, we're like the birds and the bees
But we'd rather die on our feet than keep living on our knees.

© Dynatone Publishing Co. (1967). All rights reserved.

PART TWO

You know the landlord rang my front door bell
I let it ring for a long, long spell
I went to the window
I peeked through the blind
I asked him to tell me what was on his mind—
He said, "Money, honey . . ."

—JESSE STONE

Jesse Stone

Money, Honey

You know the landlord rang my front door bell
I let it ring for a long, long spell
I went to the window
I peeked through the blind
I asked him to tell me what was on his mind—
He said, "Money, honey, uh-huh-uh, money, honey. Money, honey,
If you want to get along with me."
Well I screamed and I hollered
I was so hard pressed
I called the woman that I love the best
I finally got my baby 'bout half past three
She said, "I'd like to know what you want with me."
I said, "Money, honey, uh-huh-uh, money, honey. Money, honey,
If you want to get along with me."
Well she said, "Tell me baby what's wrong with you,
From this day on our romance is through."
I said, "Tell me baby, face to face—
How could another man take my place?"
She said, "Money, honey, uh-huh-uh, money, honey. Money, honey,
If you want to get along with me."
Well I've learned a lesson and now I know
The sun may shine and the winds may blow
The women may come and the women may go
But before I say "I love you so,"
I want money, honey, uh-huh-uh, money, honey. Money, honey,
If you want to get along with me.

Copyright © 1953 by Walden Music, Inc., 1841 Broadway, New York, N.Y. 10023.

Antoine Domino/Dave Bartholomew

Blue Monday

Blue Monday, oh, here's blue Monday
Got to work like a slave all day
Here comes Tuesday, oh hard Tuesday
I'm so tired I got no time to play
Here comes Wednesday, I'm beat to my socks
My girl calls and I tell her that I'm out
'Cause Thursday is a hard working day
And Friday I get my pay
Saturday morning, oh Saturday morning
All my tiredness has gone away
Find my money, and my honey
Then I'm out on the street to play
Sunday morning my head is bad
But it's worth it for the time that I've had
But I've got to get my rest
'Cause Monday is a mess.

© 1957 Travis Music Company. Used by permission.

The Silhouettes

Get a Job

Sha da da da sha da da da da
Sha da da da sha da da da da
Sha da da da sha da da da da
Sha da da da sha da da da da
Yip yip yip yip yip yip yip yip
Mum mum mum mum mum mum
Get a job
Sha da da da sha da da da da
Ev'ry morning about this time
She get me out of my bed a-crying get a job
After breakfast ev'ryday she throws a warning glance my way
And never fails to say get a job
Sha da da da sha da da da da
Sha da da da sha da da da da
Sha da da da sha da da da da
Sha da da da sha da da da da

Yip yip yip yip yip yip yip yip
Mum mum mum mum mum mum
Get a job
Sha da da da sha da da da da
And when I get the paper I read it thru and thru
And my girl never fails to say
If there is any work for me
And when I go back to the house I hear the woman's mouth
Preaching and a-crying tell me that I'm lying 'bout a job
That I never could find
Sha da da da sha da da da da
Sha da da da sha da da da da

© 1957 Ulysses & Bagby Music. © 1958 Wildcat Music and Ulysses & Bagby Music. Reprinted by permission of the publishers, Wildcat Music, Inc., and Kae Williams Music, Inc.

Sha da da da sha da da da da
Sha da da da sha da da da da
Yip yip yip yip yip yip yip yip
Mum mum mum mum get a job
Sha da da da sha da da da da
Sha da da da sha da da da da.

Al Smith/Luther Dixon

Big Boss Man

Big boss man, can't you hear me when I call
Big boss man, can't you hear me when I call
Can't you hear me when I call
Well you ain't so big
You know you're just tall that's all, all right.

You've got me working boss man
Working around the clock
I want a little drink of water
But you won't let me stop
Big boss man, now can't you hear me when I call
I said you ain't so big
You know you're just tall that's all
Big boss man, why can't you hear me when I call all right
You know you ain't so big
I said you're just tall that's all, all right.

I'm gonna get me a boss man
One gonna treat me right
Work hard in the daytime
Rest easy at night
Big boss man, can't you hear me when I call
I said you ain't so big
You're just tall that's all.

© 1960, 1967 Conrad Music, a division of Arc Music Corp.

Bill Anderson

Po' Folks

There a whole lotta people lookin' down their noses at me
'Cause I didn't come from a wealthy family
There was ten of us living in a two-room shack
On the bank of the river, by the railroad track
And we kept chickens in a pen in the back
And ev'rybody said we was po' folks.

My daddy was a farmer but all he ever raised was us
Dug a forty-foot well, struck thirty-six gallons of dust
The salvation army gave us clothes to wear
A man from the county came to cut our hair
We lived next door to a millionaire
But we wasn't nothin' but po' folks.

We was po' folks livin' in a rich folks world. We sure was
a hungry bunch
If the wolf had ever come to our front door he'd a had to
brought a picnic lunch.

My granddaddy's pension was a dollar and thirty-three
cents
That was ten dollars less than the landlord wanted for
rent
The landlord's letters got nasty indeed
He wrote, "Git out!" But paw couldn't read
And he was too broke to even pay heed
But that's how it is when you're po' folks.

But we had something in our house money can't buy
Kept us warm in the winter, cool when the sun was high
For whenever we didn't have food enough

© Copyright 1961 Tree Publishing Co., Inc., and Champion Music Corp. Reprinted by permission of the publishers.

And the howling winds would get pretty rough
We patched the cracks and set the table with love
'Cause that's what you do when you're po' folks
And we wasn't nothin' but po' folks.

Harlan Howard

Busted

My bills are all due and the baby needs shoes, and I'm
busted
Cotton is down to a quarter a pound, but I'm busted
I got a cow that went dry and a hen that won't lay
And a big stack of bills that gets bigger each day
The county's gonna haul my belongings away, 'cause I'm
busted
I went to my brother to ask for a loan, 'cause I'm busted
I hate to beg like a dog without his bone, but I'm busted
My brother said, "There ain't a thing I can do
My wife and kids are all down with the flu
And I was just thinking of calling on you, and I'm busted"
Well I am no thief but a man can go wrong, when he's
busted
The food that we canned all last summer is gone, and I'm
busted
The fields are all bare and the cotton won't grow
Me and my family got to pack up and go
But I'll make a living, just where I don't know
'Cause I'm busted
I'm broke . . . no bread . . . I mean like nothin' . . . forget
it . . .

© 1962 Pamper Music, Inc. All rights reserved. Reprinted by permission of copyright owner.

Lowell Fulsom/Jimmy McCracklin

Tramp

Carla: Tramp
Otis: What'd you call me?
Carla: Tramp. You don't wear continental clothes or stetson hats
Otis: I'll tell you one doggone thing. It makes me feel good to know one thing, I'm a lover
Carla: It's a matter of opinion, baby
Otis: That's all right, mama was, papa too. I'm an only child and loving is all I know how to do

Carla: You know what, Otis?
Otis: What?
Carla: You're country
Otis: That's all right
Carla: You're straight from the Georgia woods
Otis: That's good
Carla: You know what you wear, overalls, big old brogan shoes, and you need a haircut, tramp
Otis: Haircut, woman you're too—oooo. I'm a lover, mama was, grandmama too, papa too. Well I'm the only son-of-a-gun this side of the sun

Otis: Tramp
Carla: That's right, that's what you are—You know what, Otis? I don't care what you say, you're still a tramp
Otis: What?
Carla: That's right, you haven't even got a fat bank roll in your pocket. You probably haven't even got 25¢
Otis: I got 6 Cadillacs, 5 Lincolns, 4 Fords, 6 Mercurys, 3 T-Birds, Mustang—oo. I'm a lover, my mama was, my papa too. I'm the only son-of-a-gun this side of the sun

© Copyright 1967 by Modern Music.

Carla: You're a tramp, Otis
Otis: I'm not
Carla: I don't care what you say, you're still a tramp
Otis: Don't call me that
Carla: Look-a here. You ain't got no money
Otis: I got everything
Carla: You can't buy me all those minks and sables and all the stuff I want
Otis: I can buy you moose, rat, frog, squirrel, rabbit, anything you want, woman
Carla: Look, you can go out in the Georgia woods and catch them, baby
Otis: Oh, but you goofed it good
Carla: You're still a tramp
Otis: I'm not
Carla: Tramp, Otis, you're just a tramp
Otis: That's all right, my mama was too . . .
Carla: You wear overalls, you need a haircut, baby— Cut off some of that hair
Otis: I don't care at all.

Laura Nyro

Poverty Train

Last call for the poverty train
Last call for the poverty train
It looks good and dirty
On shiny light strip
And if you don't get beat
You got yourself a trip
You can see the walls roar
See your brains on the floor
Become God
Become cripple
Become funky
And split
Why was I born—
I just saw the Devil
And he's smilin' at me
I heard my bones cry
"Devil, why's it got to be?"
Devil played with my brother
Devil drove my mother
Now the tears in the gutter
Are floodin' the sea
Why was I born—
Oh baby
It looks good and dirty
Them shiny lights glow
A million night tramps
Tricks and tracks
Will come and go
You're starvin' today
But who cares anyway
Baby, it feels like I'm dyin'
Now

© 1967 Tuna Fish Music, Inc. All rights reserved.

I swear there's somethin' better than
Gettin' off on sweet cocaine
It feels so good
It feels so good
Gettin' off the poverty train
Mornin' . . .

Ray Stevens

Mr. Businessman

Itemize the things you covet
As you squander through your life
Bigger cars, bigger houses
Term insurance for your wife
Tuesday evenings with your harlot
And on Wednesdays it's your Charlatan analyst
He's high upon your list

You've got air-conditioned sinuses
And dark disturbing doubt about
Religion and you keep those cards and
Letters goin' out
While your secretary's tempting you
Your morals are exempting you from guilt and shame
Heaven knows you're not to blame

You better take care of business, Mr. Businessman
If you can
Before it's too late—and you throw your life away

Did you see your children growing up today
And did you hear the music of their laughter
As they set about to play
Did you catch the fragrance of those
Roses in your garden
Did the morning sunlight warm your soul
And brighten up your day
Do you qualify to be alive
Or is the limit of your senses so
As only to survive

Copyright 1968 by Ahab Music Company.

Spending counterfeit incentive
Wasting precious time and health
Placing value on the worthless
Disregarding priceless wealth
You can wheel and deal the best of them
And steal it from the rest of them
You know the score
Eighty-six proof anesthetic crutches
Prop you to the top
Where the smiles are all synthetic
And the ulcers never stop
When they take that final inventory
Yours will be the same sad story
Everywhere
No one will really care
No one more lonely than
This rich important man
Let's have your autograph
Endorse your epitaph

You better take care of business, Mr. Businessman
What's your plan
Get down to business, Mr. Businessman
If you can.

PART THREE

They've been so long on Lonely Street
They never will go back

—ELVIS PRESLEY/MAE AXTON/TOMMY DURDEN

Jerry Leiber/Mike Stoller

Jailhouse Rock

The warden threw a party in the country jail.
The prison band was there and they began to wail.
The band was jumpin' and the joint began to swing.
You should've heard those knocked out jailbirds sing.

Let's rock! Let's rock!
Ev'rybody in the whole cell block
Was a dancin' to the jailhouse rock!

Spider Murphy played the tenor saxophone.
Little Joe was blowin' on the slide trombone.
The drummer boy from Illinois went crash, boom, bang!
The whole rhythm section was the purple gang.

Number forty-seven said to number three:
You're the cutest jailbird I ever did see.
I sure would be delighted with your company.
Come on and do the jailhouse rock with me.

The sad sack was a-sittin' on a block of stone,
Way over in the corner weeping all alone.
The warden said: Hey, buddy, don't you be no square.
If you can't find a partner, use a wooden chair!
Let's rock,

Shifty Henry said to Bugs: For Heaven's sake,
No one's lookin'; now's our chance to make a break.
Bugsy turned to Shifty and he said: Nix, nix;
I wanna stick around a while and get my kicks.
Let's rock.

© 1957 by Elvis Presley Music, Inc., and Hill and Range Songs, Inc. Used by permission.

Felice Bryant/Boudleaux Bryant

Take a Message to Mary

These are the words of a frontier lad
Who lost his love when he turned bad.
Take a message to Mary
But don't tell her where I am.
Take a message to Mary
But don't say I'm in a jam.
You can tell her I had to see the world,
Tell her that my ship set sail.
You can say she'd better not wait for me
But don't tell her I'm in jail.
Oh, don't tell her I'm in jail.
Take a message to Mary
But don't tell her what I've done.
Please don't mention the stagecoach
And the shot from a careless gun.
You can tell her I had to change my plans
And cancel out the wedding day,
But please don't mention my lonely cell
Where I'm gonna pine away
Until my dying day.
Take a message to Mary
But don't tell her all you know.
My heart's aching for Mary,
Lord knows I miss her so.
Just tell her I went to Timbuktu,
Tell her I'm searching for gold.
You can say she'd better find someone new
To cherish and to hold.
Oh, Lord, this cell is so cold.

© Copyright 1959 by Acuff-Rose Publications, Inc. Used with permission of the publisher.

Roger Miller

King of the Road

Trailer for sale or rent
Room to let, 50¢
No phone, no pool, no pets
I ain't got no cigarettes
Ah, but two hours of pushing broom
Buys an eight by twelve, four-bit room
I'm a man of means, by no means king of the road
Road—I know road
Every engineer on every train
All of their children and all of their names
And every handout in every town
And every lock that ain't locked when no one's around
I sing
Trailer for sale or rent
Room to let, 50¢
Third boxcar, midnight train
Destination, Bangor, Maine
Old wore out suit and shoes
I don't pay no union dues
I smoke old stogies I have found
Short, but not too big around
I'm a man of means, by no means
King of the road.

© Copyright 1964 by Tree Publishing Co., Inc. Reprinted by permission of the publisher.

Curly Putman

Green, Green Grass of Home

The old home town looks the same as I step
down from the train
And there to meet me is my Mama and Papa
And down the road I look and there runs Mary
hair of gold and lips like cherries
It's good to touch the green, green grass of home
Yes they'll all come to meet me arms a-reaching
smiling sweetly
It's good to touch the green, green grass of home

The old house is still standing tho' the paint
is cracked and dry
And there's that old oak tree that I used to play on
Down the lane I walk with my sweet Mary
hair of gold and lips like cherries
It's good to touch the green, green grass of home

Then I awake and look around me at the gray walls
that surround me
And I realize that I was only dreaming
For there's a guard and there's a sad old Padre
arm and arm we'll walk
Again I'll touch the green, green grass of home

Yes they'll all come to see me in the shade of that
old oak tree
As they lay me 'neath the green, green grass of home.

© Copyright 1965 by Tree Publishing Co., Inc. Reprinted by permission of the publisher.

Elvis Presley/Mae Axton/Tommy Durden

Heartbreak Hotel

Now since my baby left me
I've found a new place to dwell
Down at the end of Lonely Street
At Heartbreak Hotel
I'm so lonely
I'm so lonely
I'm so lonely I could die
And though it's always crowded
You still can find some room
For broken-hearted lovers
To cry there in the gloom
And be so lonely
O so lonely
Be so lonely they could die
The bellhop's tears keep flowing
The desk clerk's dressed in black
They've been so long on Lonely Street
They never will go back
And they're so lonely
O they're so lonely
They're so lonely they pray to die
So if your baby leaves you
And you have a tale to tell
Just take a walk down Lonely Street
To Heartbreak Hotel
Where you'll be so lonely
And I'll be so lonely
We'll be so lonely we could die.

© Copyright 1966 by Tree Publishing Co., Inc. Reprinted by permission of the publisher.

Tim Hardin

The Lady Came from Baltimore

The lady came from Baltimore
All she wore was lace
She didn't know that I was poor
She never saw my place
I was there to steal her money
To take her rings and run
Then I fell in love with the lady
And got away with none.

The lady's name was Susan Moore
Her daddy read the law
She didn't know that I was poor
And moved outside the law
Daddy said I was a thief
Didn't marry her for love
But I was Susan's truly
And married her for love.

I was there to steal her money
To take her rings and run
Then I fell in love with the lady
And got away with none.

The house she lived in had a wall
To keep the robbers out
She never stopped to think at all
That's what I knew about
I was there to steal her money
To take her rings and run
Then I fell in love with the lady
And got away with none

© Copyright 1967 by Faithful Virtue Music Co., Inc. Used by permission. All rights reserved.

Then I fell in love with the lady
And got away with none.

People Are Strange

People are strange when you're a stranger,
Faces look ugly when you're alone.
Women seem wicked when you're unwanted,
Streets are uneven when you're down.
When you're strange
Faces come out of the rain
When you're strange
No one remembers your name
When you're strange
When you're strange
When you're strange.

© 1967 by Nipper Music Company, Inc. All rights reserved.

PART FOUR

First a boy and a girl meet each other
Then they sit down to talk for a while
In their hearts they want each other for lovers
As each step draws them closer to the aisle

—BILLY DAWN SMITH/STUART WIENER

Robert Blackwell/McKinley "Lil" Millet

All Around the World

All around the world, rock and roll is all they play
All around the world, rock and roll is all they play
You can hear those jukebox jumpin'
All night long and through the day
All the flat-top cats with their rock and roll queens
Just a rockin' and a rollin' in their red and blue jeans
All around the world, rock and roll is all they play
You can hear those jukebox jumpin'
All night long and through the day
Ain't never no time for romance
They only want to dance
The people all holler when they hit the floor—
"Go, cat, go!"
All around the world, rock and roll is all they play
You can hear those jukebox jumpin'
All night long and through the day
They do the bop, the Texas hop
Shim-sham-shimmy, and they never never stop
All around the world, rock and roll is all they play
You can hear those jukebox jumpin'
All night long and through the day.

© 1956 Venice Music, Inc. Reprinted by permission of the publisher.

Ellas McDaniel

Who Do You Love?

I walk forty-seven miles of barbed wire
I use a cobra snake for a necktie
I got a brand new house by the roadside
Made out of rattlesnake hide
I got a brand new chimney made up on top
Made out of a human skull
Now come on, take a little walk with me, Arlene
And tell me
Who do you love?
Who do you love?
Tombstone hand and graveyard mind
I'm just twenty-two and I don't mind dying
Who do you love?
I go out on the town, use a rattlesnake whip
Take it easy, Arlene, don't give me no lip
Who do you love?
The night was dark, the sky was blue
Down the alley an ice wagon flew
Hit a bump and somebody screamed
You should have heard just what I seen
Who do you love?
Arlene took me by my hand
She said "Oowee Bo, you know I understand."
Who do you love?
Who do you love?

© 1956, 1963 Arc Music Corp.

Felice Bryant/Boudleaux Bryant

Wake Up, Little Susie

Wake up, little Susie, wake up
Wake up, little Susie, wake up
We both been sound asleep
Wake up, little Susie, and weep
The movie's over, it's four o'clock
And we're in trouble deep
Wake up, little Susie
Wake up, little Susie
Well, what are we gonna tell your mama?
What are we gonna tell your pa?
What are we gonna tell our friends when they say "Ooh-la-la"?
Wake up, little Susie
Wake up, little Susie
Well, I told your mama that you'd be in by ten
Susie baby, looks like we goofed again
Wake up, little Susie
Wake up, little Susie
We gotta go home
Wake up, little Susie, wake up
Wake up, little Susie, wake up
The movie wasn't so hot
It didn't have much of a plot
We fell asleep, our goose is cooked
Our reputation is shot
Wake up, little Susie
Wake up, little Susie
We gotta go home.

© 1957 Acuff-Rose Publications, Inc. (for the world except the United States). © 1957 House of Bryant (United States only). Used pursuant to authority granted by the publishers.

Billy Dawn Smith/Stuart Wiener

To the Aisle

First a boy and a girl meet each other
Then they sit down to talk for a while.
In their hearts they want each other for lovers
As each step draws them nearer to the aisle.
They might start with a simple conversation
Like, "Darling, would you put me on trial?"
Then they kiss and feel a certain sensation
As each step draws them nearer to the aisle.
He asks, "Do you love me?"
She answers, "I do"
She wants to know if his love will be true.
A ring on her finger will prove that he cares
Then he takes her hand so gently
And gives her one to wear.
Then the light in her eyes starts a-glowing
And the tears would conquer her smile.
In her heart he knows the joy is overflowing
While each step draws them nearer to the aisle.

© Copyright 1957 by Wemar Music Corporation.

Bobby Freeman

Do You Wanna Dance?

Well, do you wanna dance and hold my hand,
Tell me I'm your lover man,
O baby, do you wanna dance?
Well, do you wanna dance and make romance,
Squeeze me all through the night,
O baby, do you wanna dance?
Well, do you wanna dance, under the moonlight,
Squeeze me all through the night,
O baby, do you wanna dance?
Well, do you wanna dance and hold my hand,
Squeeze me, say I'm your lover man,
O baby, do you wanna dance?
Well, do you wanna dance and to make romance?
Kiss and squeeze—yes!
Do you wanna dance?
Do you, do you, do you, do you wanna dance?
Do you, do you, do you, do you wanna dance?
Do you, do you, do you, do you wanna dance?

Copyright © 1958 Clockus Music, Inc.

Barry Mann/Cynthia Weil

Saturday Night at the Movies

Well, Saturday night at eight o'clock I know where I'm
gonna go
I'm gonna pick up my baby and take her to the picture show
Everybody in the neighborhood is dressin' up to be there
too
And we're gonna have a ball just like we always do
A Saturday night at the movies
Who cares what picture you see
When you're huggin' with your baby
In the last row in the balcony
Well, there's technicolor and cinemascope
A cast out of Hollywood
And the popcorn from the candy stand
Makes it all seem twice as good
There's always lots of pretty girls
With figures they don't try to hide
But they never can compare
To the girl sitting by my side
A Saturday night at the movies
Who cares what picture you see
When you're huggin' with your baby
In the last row in the balcony
Movies are better than ever
And just as dark as before
And Saturday night when you're with your baby
Who could ask for anything more?
A Saturday night at the movies
Who cares what picture you see
When you're huggin' with your baby
In the last row in the balcony.

© Copyright 1964 by Screen Gems–Columbia Music, Inc., New York, N.Y. Used by permission. Reproduction prohibited.

Joe Tex

The Love You Save (May Be Your Own)

People I've been misled
And I've been afraid
I've been hit in the head
And left for dead
I've been abused
And I've been accused
I've been refused a piece of bread
But I never in my life before
Seen so many love affairs go wrong
As they do today
I want you to stop!
Find out what's wrong
Get it right
Or just leave love alone
Because the love
You save today
May very well
Be your own.

Listen to me—
I been pushed around
I been lost and found
I been given till sundown
To get out of town
I been taken outside
And I been brutalized
And I had to always be the one
To smile and apologize
But I ain't never
In my life before
Seen so many love affairs go wrong

© Copyright 1965 by Tree Publishing Co., Inc. Reprinted by permission of the publisher.

As they do today
I want you to stop!
Find out what's wrong
Get it right
Or just leave love alone
Because the love
You save today
May very well
Be your own.

Jim Webb

By the Time I Get to Phoenix

By the time I get to Phoenix
She'll be risin'
She'll find the note I left there
Hangin' on her door
And she will laugh when she reads the part that says I'm
leavin'
'Cause I've left that girl so many times before
By the time I make Albuquerque she'll be workin'
She'll probably stop at lunch to give me a call
But she'll just hear the empty phone just keep on ringin'
off the wall
And that is all
By the time I make Oklahoma she'll be sleepin'
She'll turn softly as she lies and calls my name out low
And she will cry to think that I would really leave her
Tho' time and time again I've tried to tell her so
She didn't know that I would really go.

© 1967 Rivers Music Co. All rights reserved. Used with permission.

Wyatt Day

Automatic Love

It used to be, when you're feeling lonely
You'd go right out and find a little girl
But now they have a new machine
The prettiest little thing you've ever seen
It's electronic
It's automatic
And it makes a humming sound
They put your name upon a card your age your weight
your height
Your sight your ears and what you eat for breakfast food
Your favorite car your birthstone and your hat
And that my friend is not the end your schooling and
your IQ
Have you ever been arrested if so why
Your favorite film your glove size and your faith
And then it's all notated, written down and perforated
And they drop your little card into a slot
I went to the office, filled out an application
I paid four dollars to make a reservation
The man was very kind, he seemed to understand
He said it can't go wrong, it never makes mistakes
It's electronic
It's automatic
And it makes a humming sound
I feel so good
I feel secure
It's going to find me a girl
Well I woke up on Monday morning
Received a postcard phrased discretely
It said I had a date with a certain Agnes Snow
Her name, address, a place for me to go

© 1967 by Wyatt H. Day, Wild Indigo Music, and Sweetpea Music, 850 Seventh Avenue, New York, N.Y. 10019.

I was ecstatic, my thoughts erratic
And I made a humming sound
Called her on the telephone
She's so sweet
We met and then she swept me off my feet
Three weeks more was all it took
To make me ask her to be mine
She said yes
We went right out to find a justice of the peace
Knocked at the door, it opened to reveal
The prettiest little thing you've ever seen
An automatic, electronic machine.

Lou Reed

All Tomorrow's Parties

And what costume shall the poor girl wear
To all tomorrow's parties?
A hand-me-down dress from who knows where
To all tomorrow's parties.
And where will she go
And what shall she do
When midnight comes around?
She'll turn once more to Sunday's clown
And cry behind the door.
And what costume shall the poor girl wear
To all tomorrow's parties?
Why, silks and linens of yesterday's gowns
To all tomorrow's parties.
And what will she do with Thursday's rags
When Monday comes around?
She'll turn once more to Sunday's clown
And cry behind the door.
And what costume shall the poor girl wear
To all tomorrow's parties?
For Thursday's child is Sunday's clown
For whom none will go mourning.
A blackened shroud, a hand-me-down gown
Of rags and silk, a costume
Fit for one who sits and cries
For all tomorrow's parties.

© The Velvet Underground M-G-M.

Brian Wilson/Mike Love

I'd Love Just Once to See You

I'm doing this and I'm doing that
And I'm walking the floor
Drink a little of this and eat a little of that
And poke my head out the door
I keep thinking I'm a-wasting the night away
I wouldn't mind if I could get with you right away
Oh, honey, I don't know how long it's been
But this feeling's building up inside again
I wash the dishes and I rinse up the sink
Like a busy bee
I make up a song as I'm walking along
No one's watching me
I wish that you were here to help me dry
When's the last time you baked me a pie?
You had a way of making it come alive
It's not too late for you to take a drive
It's not too late—
I'd love just once to see you
I'd love just once to see you
I'd love just once to see you in the nude.

© 1968 by Sea of Tunes Publishing Co., Inc.

PART FIVE

Come Friday noon about half past three
I drop my books and my misery

—JOSEPH ROISTER/FRANK J. GUIDA

Julius Dixon/Ollie Jones/Alan Freed

Teenage Meeting

Put out the cat, lock the door
There's a teenage meeting at the candy store
Gonna rock it up right tonight, gonna rock it up right tonight
Gonna ramble, gonna scramble, gotta dance to my heart's delight
Here comes Lilly popping bubble gum
Look at Rosie having loads of fun
Hot dogs crackin' with soda pop
Jukebox screamin', 'bout to blow his top
Out of my way, here I go
To the teenage meeting at the candy store.

Smiling faces beaming everywhere
Jack and Mary dancing on their chairs
When the meeting really starts to rock
Old Man Thornton's pointing at the clock
Crew cut Willy brought Pigtail Ann
Hey, hot Dilly, but I've got Jan
Meeting to order, call the roll
Everybody's present, let's rock and roll
Who rang the bell? What a gas!
Look again, Mister, your clock is fast
Got to get going, can't be late
Got a sweet little cutie who just won't wait. . . .

© 1955 by Wemar Music Corporation.

Chuck Berry

School Day

Up in the morning and out to school
The teacher is teaching the Golden Rule
American history, practical math
You study them hard, hoping to pass
Working your fingers right down to the bone
And the guy behind you won't leave you alone
Ring, ring goes the bell
The cook in the lunchroom's ready to sell
You're lucky if you can find a seat
You're fortunate if you have time to eat
Back in the classroom—open your books
Even the teacher don't know
How mean she looks
Soon as three o'clock rolls around
You finally lay your burden down
Close up your books and get out of your seat
Down the halls and into the street
Up to the corner and around the bend
Right to the juke joint you go in
Drop the coin right into the slot
You've gotta hear something that's really hot
With the one you love you're making romance
All day long you've been wanting to dance
Feeling the music from head to toe
Round and round and round you go
Hail, hail rock and roll
Remember it from the days of old
Rock, rock, rock and roll
The beat of the drums loud and bold
Long live rock and roll
The feeling is there, body and soul!

© 1957 Arc Music Corp.

Jerry Leiber/Mike Stoller

Yakety-Yak

Take out the papers and the trash
Or you don't get no spending cash
If you don't scrub that kitchen floor
You ain't gonna rock'n' roll no more
Yakety-yak. Don't talk back
Just finish cleaning up your room
Let's see that dust fly with that broom
Get all that garbage out of sight
Or you don't go out Friday night
Yakety-yak. Don't talk back
You just put on your coat and hat
And walk yourself to the laundromat
And when you finish doing that
Bring in the dog and put out the cat
Yakety-yak. Don't talk back
Don't you give me no dirty looks
Your father's hip, he knows what cooks
Just tell your hoodlum friends outside
You ain't got time to take a ride
Yakety-yak.
Don't talk back.

© 1958 Tiger Music, Inc. Used by permission.

Sid Tepper/Roy C. Bennett

School Dance

I really had the craziest dream last night,
About a school dance;
A rock and roll band,
And the gym was jammed,
For the school dance.
You and I were there,
Oo, what a happy pair,
King and queen of the whole affair,
At the school dance.
Ev'rytime I danced with you, baby,
I could hear my heart a-thumpin',
The principal was dancing with the teachers,
And the gym was really jumpin'.
Boys (girls) buzzed 'round your throne,
Like bees 'round a honeycomb,
But you had eyes for me alone,
At the school dance.
My greatest thrill came when the dance was through;
I (you) walked you (me) home,
And got my very first kiss from you.
One thing that I'm sad about,
It's just a dream I had,
About a school dance.
Tomorrow night there's gonna be,
A rockin', rollin', jamboreein' school dance.
Baby, come with me,
And for real we'll be doing,
All the things we did in my dream,
At the school dance.

Copyright © 1958 by Planetary Music Publishing Corp., 17 West 60th Street, New York, N.Y. 10023. All rights reserved. International copyright secured.

Joseph Roister/Frank J. Guida

High School U.S.A.

Come Friday noon about half past three
I drop my books and my misery
Stroll up and down to the soda shop
Drop a coin in the old jukebox
Well now, lookin' all around what did I see
Ev'ry school kid there could ever be
They come from:

Well, come Saturday morning they were still going strong
They been a-rockin' and a-rollin' all night long
No time to study on their ABC's
They're gettin' their lessons on the birds and the bees
Yeah, all across the floor they are doin' the hop
Ev'rybody doin' that-a High School bop
They come from:

Copyright 1949 by Progressive Music Publishing Co., Inc. Used by permission.

Brian Wilson

Be True to Your School

When some loud braggard tries to put me down
And says his school is great
I tell him right away, "Now what's the matter buddy,
Ain't you heard of my school? It's number one in the
state."
So be true to your school
Just like you would to your girl or guy
Be true to your school
Let your colors fly
Be true to your school—
I got a letterman's sweater with a letter in front
I got for football and track
I'm proud to wear it now
When I cruise around the other parts of the town
I got my decal in back
So be true to your school
Just like you would to your girl or guy
Be true to your school
Let your colors fly
Be true to your school—
On Friday we'll be jacked up on the football field
And we'll be ready to fight
We're gonna smash 'em now
My girl will be putting on her pompoms now
And she'll be yelling tonight
So be true to your school
Just like you would to your girl or guy
Be true to your school
Let your colors fly
Be true to your school—
Rah, rah, rah, be true to your school. . . .

© 1963 by Sea of Tunes Publishing Co., Inc.

Burt Jones

Don't Be a Dropout

Now a good friend of mine
Sat with me and he cried
Told me a story, I know he hadn't lied
Said he went for a job
And then the Man said
"Without an education
You might as well be dead
Now don't get me wrong,"
He said, "It's not who you are
But people come to me
From near and far
I do just work
And I follow my rules
I didn't have an education
So I had to go back to school"
My friend told all his buddies
That he loved so well
And of their personal troubles
I do not tell
Now these guys didn't seem good
And they didn't seem bad
They didn't seem so happy
And I know they weren't sad
But the point is this—
That they followed the rules
They got an education
And they all finished school
Now underneath his tears
I could see the true fact
When he dropped out of school
He never never went back
Got to, got to, got to listen now

© Dynatone Publishing Co. (1967). All rights reserved.

Without an education
You might as well be dead
So one day he got tired
Of his little spending change
So he looked up his friends
And checked their pay range
When he got there the clerk found
That he was a drag
'Cause man, they were clean
And his clothes were like rags
One was a businessman with plenty of dough
Had his thing so set up
He knew he couldn't blow
The other had his job
So up tight
Had his whole family and his kids
Out of sight
Well, what made him so hurt
That these were his friends and he was a drag
They looked at him
And he was in the same old bag
For his friends they worked real hard
When they worked their way through
Now he realized
He should have done the same thing too
They kept on pushing
When the going was tough
And now they know
That things don't seem so rough
So kids, stay in school
And don't be a drag
Take a fool's advice
And stay out of that bag.

PART SIX

This little modified pon-ton
Has got plenty of style

—JOHN WILKIN

Jerry Leiber/Mike Stoller

Black Denim Trousers and Motorcycle Boots

He wore black denim trousers and motorcycle boots
And a black leather jacket with an eagle on the back
He had a hopped-up cycle that took off like a gun
That fool was the terror of Highway 101
Well, he never washed his face and he never combed his
hair
He had axle grease embedded underneath his fingernails
On the muscle of his arm was a red tattoo
A picture of a heart saying "Mother, I love you"
He had a pretty girlfriend by the name of Mary Lou
But he treated her just like he treated all the rest
And everybody pitied her and everybody knew
He loved that doggone motorcycle best

He wore black denim trousers and motorcycle boots
And a black leather jacket with an eagle on the back
He had a hopped-up cycle that took off like a gun
That fool was the terror of Highway 101
Mary Lou, poor girl, she pleaded and she begged him not
to leave
She said "I've got a feeling if you ride tonight I'll grieve"
But her tears were shed in vain and her every word was lost
In the rumble of his engine and the smoke from his exhaust
He took off like the devil, there was fire in his eyes
He said "I'll go a thousand miles before the sun can rise"
But he hit a screaming diesel that was California bound
And when they cleared the wreckage all they found—
Was his black denim trousers and his motorcycle boots
And a black leather jacket with an eagle on the back
But they couldn't find the cycle that took off like a gun
And they never found the terror of Highway 101.

© 1955 Quintet Music. Used by permission.

Chuck Berry/Russ Fratto/Alan Freed

Mabellene

Mabellene, why can't you be true?
O Mabellene, why can't you be true?
You done started back doing the things you used to do—
As I was a motivatin' over the hill
I saw Mabellene in a Coupe de Ville
Cadillac rolling on the open road
Nothing outruns my V-8 Ford
Cadillac doing about ninety-five
Bumper to bumper, rolling side by side
Mabellene, why can't you be true?
Mabellene, why can't you be true?
You done started back doing the things you used to do—
Cadillac pulled up ahead of the Ford
My Ford got hot and wouldn't do no more
Then it got cloudy and started to rain
I tooted my horn for the passing lane
Rainwater rolled all under my hood
I knew it was doing my motor good
Mabellene, why can't you be true?
O Mabellene, why can't you be true?
You done started back doing the things you used to do—
Motor cooled down, heat went down
That's when I heard that highway sound
Cadillac sitting like a ton of lead
One hundred and ten, half a mile ahead
Cadillac looks like it's sitting still
And I caught Mabellene at the top of the hill—
Mabellene, why can't you be true?
O Mabellene, why can't you be true?
You done started back doing the things you used to do.

© 1955 Arc Music Corp.

Jean Surrey/Red Surrey

Teen Angel

That fateful night the car was stalled
Upon the railroad track
I pulled you out and we were safe
But you went running back.

Teen angel can you hear me
Teen angel can you see me
Are you somewhere up above
And am I still your own true love?

What was it you were looking for
That took your life that night
They said they found my high school ring
Clutched in your fingers tight.

Just sweet sixteen and now you're gone
They've taken you away
I'll never kiss your lips again
They buried you today.

© Copyright 1959 by Acuff-Rose Publications, Inc. Used with permission of the publisher.

Brian Wilson/Roger Christian

The Ballad of Ole' Betsey

She was born in '32
And was she ever pretty
She rode a freight train west
All the way from Detroit City
Betsey's seen more places than I'll ever hope to see
Betsey's been more loyal than any friend could be
With some she traveled far
With others it was slow
Betsey's seen them all
She's seen them come and go
She must have had some favorites
Before I finally met her
And now that she's my car
They'd better just forget her
Betsey was a lady and that she will remain
Betsey took some beatings but she never once complained
She had a classic beauty
That everyone could see
I was the last to meet her
But she gave her life to me
She may be rusted iron
But to me she's solid gold
And I just can't hold the tears back
'Cause Betsey's growing old. . . .

© 1963 by Sea of Tunes Publishing Co., Inc.

Jeff Barry

Tell Laura I Love Her

Laura and Tommy were lovers
He wanted to give her everything;
Flowers, presents, and most of all
A wedding ring!
He saw a sign for a stock car race
A thousand-dollar prize it read;
He couldn't get Laura on the phone,
So to her mother Tommy said:
"Tell Laura I love her!
Tell Laura I need her!
Tell Laura I may be late,
I've something to do that cannot wait."
He drove his car to the racing grounds,
He was the youngest driver there;
The crowd roared as they started the race,
Round the track they drove at a deadly pace!
No one knows what happened that day,
How his car overturned in flames
But as they pulled him from the twisted wreck,
With his dying breath they heard him say:
"Tell Laura I love her!
Tell Laura I need her!
Tell Laura not to cry,
My love for her will never die!"
(Spoken): Now in the chapel Laura prays
For her Tommy who passed away
It was just for Laura he lived and died,
Alone in the chapel she can hear him cry:
"Tell Laura I love her!
Tell Laura I need her!
Tell Laura not to cry,
My love for her will never die!"

© Edward B. Marks Music Corporation. Used by permission.

John Wilkin

GTO

Little GTO
You're really looking fine
Three deuces and a four-speed
And a 389
Listen to her taching up now
Listen to her whine
Come on and turn it on, wind it up, blow it out, GTO
You ought to see her on a road course
Or a quarter mile
This little modified pon-ton
Has got plenty of style
She beats the gasers and the rail jobs
Really drives them wild
Come on and turn it on, wind it up, blow it out, GTO
Gonna save all my money
And buy a GTO
Get a helmet and a roll bar
And I'll be ready to go
Take it out to Pomona
And let 'em know
That I'm the coolest thing around
Little buddy, gonna shut you down
When I turn it on, wind it up, blow it out, GTO.

© 1964 Buckhorn Music Publishers, Inc., P.O. Box 46, Nashville, Tennessee 37202. All rights reserved. International copyright secured.

PART SEVEN

He doesn't look like a movie star
He doesn't drive a Cadillac car
He sure ain't the boy I been dreaming of
But he's sure the boy I love

—BARRY MANN/CYNTHIA WEIL

Jerry Leiber/Mike Stoller

Charlie Brown

Fee fee fi fi fo fo fum
I smell smoke in the auditorium
Charlie Brown
Charlie Brown
He's a clown
That Charlie Brown
He's gonna get caught, just you wait and see
"Why's everybody always pickin' on me?"
That's him on his knees
I know it's him
Yelling "Seven-come-eleven" down in the boy's gym
Charlie Brown
Charlie Brown
He's a clown
That Charlie Brown
He's gonna get caught, just you wait and see
"Why's everybody always pickin' on me?"
Who's always writing on the wall?
Who's always goofing in the hall?
Who's always throwing spitballs?
Guess who?
"Who, me?"
Yes, you!
He walks in the classroom
Cool and slow
Who calls the English teacher Daddy-O?
Charlie Brown
Charlie Brown
He's a clown
That Charlie Brown
He's gonna get caught
Just you wait and see
"Why's everybody always pickin' on me?"

© 1959 by Tiger Music, Inc. Used by permission.

Gene Pitney

He's a Rebel

See the way he walks down the street
Watch the way he shuffles his feet
Oh, how he holds his head up high
When he goes walkin' by
He's my guy
When he holds my hand I'm so proud
'Cause he's not just one of the crowd
My baby's always the one
To try the things they've never done
And just because of that they say—
He's a rebel
And he'll never ever be
Any good
He's a rebel
'Cause he never ever does
What he should
Well, just because he doesn't do
What everybody else does
That's no reason why
I can't give him all my love
He is always good to me
Always treats me tenderly
He's not a rebel
No, no, no
He's not a rebel
No, no, no
Not to me.

If they don't like him that way
They won't like me after today

© 1962 January Music Corporation, a subsidiary of A. Schroeder Music Corporation. All rights reserved. International copyright secured.

I'll be standing right by his side
When they say he's a rebel
And he'll never ever be any good
He's a rebel
And he never ever does
What he should
Just because he doesn't do what
Everybody else does
That's no reason why
We can't share a love
He is always good to me
Good to him I'll try to be
'Cause he's not a rebel
No, no, no
He's not a rebel
No, no, no, not to me.

Barry Mann/Cynthia Weil

He's Sure the Boy I Love

I always dreamed the boy I love would come along
And he'd be tall and handsome, rich and strong
Now that boy I love has come to me
But he sure ain't the way I thought he'd be—
He doesn't look like a movie star
He doesn't drive a Cadillac car
He sure ain't the boy I been dreaming of
But he's sure the boy I love
Let me tell you now—
He'll never be a big millions man
He always buys on the installment plan
He sure ain't the boy I been dreaming of
But he's sure the boy I love
When he holds me tight
Everything's right
Crazy as it seems
I'm his, whatever he is
And I forget all of my dreams
Everybody knows—
He doesn't hang diamonds round my neck
And all he's got is unemployment checks
He sure ain't the boy I been dreaming of
But he's sure the boy I love.

© Copyright 1962, 1963 by Screen Gems–Columbia Music, Inc., New York, N.Y. Used by permission. Reproduction prohibited.

Jeff Barry/Ellie Greenwich

Out in the Streets

He don't hang around with the gang no more
And he don't do the wild things that he did before
He used to act bad
He used to, but he quit it
He makes me so sad
'Cause I know that he did it for me
(Can't you see?)
And I can see
(It's still in the streets)
His heart is out in the streets

He don't comb his hair like he did before
And he don't wear those dirty old black boots no more
But he's not the same
There's something 'bout his kissin' that tells me
He's changed
I know that something's missing inside
Something's died
His heart is out in the streets

He grew up on the sidewalk
Street lights shining above
He grew up with no one to love
He grew up on the sidewalk
He grew up running free
He grew up—and then he met me

He don't hang around with the gang no more
But, gee, he doesn't smile like he did before
I wish I didn't care
I wish I never met him

Copyright © 1965 Trio Music Co., Inc. Printed by permission.
All rights reserved. International copyright secured.

And waiting out there
I know I gotta set him free—
He's got to be out in the streets
His heart is out in the streets.

PART EIGHT

I want a girl that can love like a monkey

—TULI KUPFERBERG

John F. Young, Jr./Boyd Bennett/ Chuck Gorman

Seventeen

Seventeen, seventeen, cool and solid seventeen
Young enough to dance and sing
Old enough to get that swing
Passed sixteen, done been kissed
Graduated and got that twist
Kind of love I can't resist
At seventeen
Now, sloppy shirt, old blue jeans
Dirty shoes, by all means
Patch of blonde peroxide hair
Jukebox baby, ain't no square
Seventeen, hot rod queen
Cutest gal you've ever seen
Tell the world I'm really keen
On my hepcat doll of seventeen.

© 1955 Lois Publishing Company. Reprinted by permission of the publisher.

Sweet Little Sixteen

They're really rocking in Boston
Pittsburgh, Pa.
Deep in the heart of Texas
And round the Frisco Bay
All over St. Louis
And down in New Orleans
All the cats want to dance with
Sweet little sixteen.

Sweet little sixteen
She's just got to have
About half a million
Signed autographs
Her wallet's filled with pictures
She counts them one by one
Becomes so excited
Won't you look at her run?
"Oh Mommy, Mommy, please can I go
It's such a sight to see
Somebody steal the show,
Oh Daddy, Daddy, I beg of you
Whisper to Mommy
It's all right with you."

'Cause they'll be rocking on Bandstand
In Philadelphia, Pa.
Deep in the heart of Texas
And round the Frisco Bay
All over St. Louis
And down in New Orleans
All the cats want to dance with
Sweet little sixteen.

© 1958 Arc Music Corp.

Sweet little sixteen
She's got the grown-up blues
Tight dresses and lipstick
She's sporting high-heeled shoes
O but tomorrow morning she'll have to change her trend
And be sweet sixteen
And back in class again.

Richard Adler/Robert Allan

The Girl on Page Forty-Four

I never held her hand, never heard her voice
And I don't even know her name
But I've been hoping for a storybook romance
Ever since I took that very first glance
I'd like to get a girl from Sears and Roebuck
Like the one that I saw
Wearing short-shorts on page forty-four
I sent for lots of things from Sears and Roebuck
Spark plugs and fancy ties
Now I'd like to send for the gal
With the baby blue eyes
So tell me, what's the order number
For the cutest number in your catalogue?
Gee I need her, oh so badly
I'll spend a million kisses gladly
I'm lonely, Mr. Sears and Mr. Roebuck
Come on and send her to me
And make it Air Mail Special, C.O.D.

© 1958 International Korwin Corporation.

Jerry Leiber/Mike Stoller

Poison Ivy

She comes on like a rose
But everybody knows
She'll get you in dutch
You can look but you'd better not touch
Poison ivy, poison ivy
Late at night while you're sleepin'
Poison ivy comes a-creepin' around

She's pretty as a daisy
But look out man, she's crazy
She'll really do you in
If you let her get under your skin
Poison ivy, poison ivy
Late at night while you're sleepin'
Poison ivy comes a-creepin' around

Measles make you bumpy
And mumps'll make you lumpy
Chicken pox'll make you jump and twitch
A common cold'll fool you
And whoopin' cough'll cool you
But poison ivy, Lord'll make you itch

You're gonna need an ocean
Of calamine lotion
You'll be scratchin' like a hound
The minute you start to mess around
Poison ivy, poison ivy
Late at night while you're sleepin'
Poison ivy comes a-creepin' around. . . .

© 1959 Tiger Music, Inc. Used by permission.

Jerry Leiber/Phil Spector

Spanish Harlem

There is a rose in Spanish Harlem
A rare rose up in Spanish Harlem
It is a special one
It's never seen the sun
It only comes out when the moon is on the run
And all the stars are gleaming
It's growing in the street
Right up through the concrete
But soft and sweet and dreaming
There is a rose in Spanish Harlem
A rare rose up in Spanish Harlem
With eyes as black as coal
That look down in my soul
And start a fire there and then I lose control
I have to beg your pardon
I'm going to pick that rose
And watch her as she grows
In my garden.

© 1960 Progressive Music Publishing Co., Inc., and Trio Music.
Used by permission.

Tuli Kupferberg

Supergirl

I want a girl that can - - - - like an angel
Cook like the devil
Swing like a dancer
Work like a pony
Dream like a poet
Flow like a mountain stream
Supergirl
Supergirl
Supergirl
My Supergirl
I want a girl that can kiss like a cherry
Squeeze like a berry
Smell like an orchard
Talk like a songbird
Walk like a fountain
Touch like a flower
Sing like the leaves of grass

Supergirl
Supergirl
Supergirl
My Supergirl
I want a girl that can love like a monkey
Hug like a castle
Think like a darling
Lap like a lemon
Eat like a monster
Roll like a jug of wine

Supergirl

© 1965 Heavy Metal Music, Inc.

Supergirl
Supergirl
My Supergirl
I want a girl that can kiss like an eagle
Bend like a sapling
Bark like a beagle
Bite like a bagel
Fly like a butter
Shake like a - - - - within a - - - -

Supergirl
Supergirl
Supergirl
My Supergirl.

Brian Wilson

California Girls

Well, East Coast girls are hip
I really dig those styles they wear
And the Southern girls with the way they talk
They knock me out when I'm down there
The Midwest farmers' daughters really make you feel all
right
And the Northern girls, well the way they kiss
They keep their boyfriends warm at night
I wish they all could be California girls
I wish they all could be California girls
I wish they all could be California girls
The West Coast has the sunshine
And the girls all get so tan
I dig the French bikinis on Hawaiian girls
By a palm tree in the sand
I've been all around this great big girl
And I've seen all kinds of girls
But I couldn't wait to get back to the States
Back to the cutest girls in the world
I wish they all could be California girls.

© 1965 by Sea of Tunes Publishing Co., Inc.

20th Century Fox

Well she's fashionably lean
And she's fashionably late
She'll never rank a scene
She'll never break a date
But she's no drag
Just watch the way she walks
She's a—20th century fox
She's a—20th century fox
No tears
No fears
No ruined years
No clocks
She's a 20th century fox, now baby.

She's the queen of cool
She's the lady who waits
Since her mind left school
It never hesitates
She won't waste time on elementary talk
'Cause she's a
20th century fox
A 20th century fox
Got the world locked up
Inside a plastic box
She's a 20th century fox, yeah baby
A 20th century fox!

Copyright © 1967 by Nipper Music Company, Inc. All rights reserved.

PART NINE

Well, I quit my job down at the car wash
I left my momma a goodbye note
By sundown I'd left Kingston
With my guitar under my coat

—JERRY REED

Johnny Brandon/Jimmy Williams

Please Buy My Record

I'm a teenage singer, made me a record,
Ooh yes, and I pray it will go far,
Please, oh please, oh please buy my record,
Ooh yes, and make me a top ten star.
I wore short-shorts and I went to the hop,
Heard the cha-cha-cha and the bop,
There's Johnny and Elvis and Ricky and Sam,
So please buy my record,
Help a little girl if you can.

Now my ma and pa thought that I was a kid,
And much too young to do what I did,
But now they're excited when my record's played,
And hope that I'll someday make the Hit Parade.
Oh, I'm a teenager just like you,
Please won't you help me, here's what you do,
Write to your Deejay, send a request,
Say that my record is the one you like the best.

© Copyright 1958 by Monument Music, Inc.

Johnny B. Goode

Deep down in Louisiana close to New Orleans
Way back up in the woods among the evergreens
There stood a log cabin made of earth and wood
Where lived a country boy named Johnny B. Goode
Who never ever learned to read or write so well
But he could play a guitar just like ringing a bell
Go go, go Johnny go
Go go, go Johnny go
Go, Johnny B. Goode

He used to carry his guitar in a gunny sack
And sit beneath a tree by the railroad track
The engineer would see him sitting in the shade
Strumming out the rhythms that the driver made
The people passing by would stop and say
"O my, that country boy can play."
Go go, go Johnny go
Go go, go Johnny go
Go, Johnny B. Goode

His mother told him "Someday you will be a man,
And you will be the leader of a big old band
Many people coming from miles around
To hear you play your music when the sun goes down
Maybe some day your name will be in lights
Saying 'Johnny B. Goode Tonight.' "

© 1955 Arc Music Corp.

Bobby Bare

The All-American Boy

Gather round cats and I'll tell you a story
About how to become an all-American boy
Buy you a guitar and put it in tune
You'll be rockin' and rollin' soon
Impressin' the girls
Pickin' hot licks
And all that jazz
I got me a guitar a year ago
Learned how to play in a day or so
And all around town it was well understood
That I was knockin' 'em out like Johnny B. Goode
Hot licks
Showin' off
Number one
I practiced all day and into the night
My papa's hair was turning white
'Cause he didn't like rock and roll
He said, "You can stay, boy, but that's got to go."
He's a square
He just didn't dig me at all
So I took my guitar picks and all
Bid farewell to my poor paw
Split for Memphis where they say "you-all"
And them swingin' cats are having a ball
Session
Hot licks and all
They dug me
I was rockin' and boppin' and gettin' the breaks
The girls all said that I had what it takes
When up stepped a man with a big cigar
He said, "Come here, son, I'm gonna make you a star—

© 1966 Mayhew Music Co., Inc.

I'll put you on Bandstand
Buy you a Cadillac
Sign here, kid."
I signed my name and became a star
Havin' a ball with my guitar
Drivin' a big long Cadillac
And fightin' the girls right off of my back
They just kept a-comin'
Screaming
Yeah—they like it
So I picked my guitar with a great big grin
And the money just kept on pouring in
But then one day my Uncle Sam said (knock, knock, knock)
"Here I am.
Uncle Sam needs you, boy
I'm gonna cut your hair
Take this rifle, kid
Gimme that guitar. . . ."

Jim McGuinn/Chris Hillman

So You Want To Be a Rock and Roll Star

So you want to be a rock and roll star
Then listen now to what I say
Just get an electric guitar and take some time and learn
how to play
And when your hair's so right
And your pants are tight
It's gonna be all right

Then it's time to go downtown
To the agent man who won't let you down
Sell your soul to the company
Who are waiting there to sell plastic ware
And in a week or two if you make the charts
The girls will tear you apart
But you paid for your riches and fame
Was it all a strange game
You're a little insane
Money that came and public acclaim
Don't forget what you are
You're a rock 'n' roll star
La la la la la la la la la la la la la la.

© Copyright 1966 by Tickson Music Co.

John Sebastian

Nashville Cats

Nashville cats
Play clean as country water
Nashville cats
Play wild as mountain dew
Nashville cats
Been playin' since they'se babies
Nashville cats
It worked before they're two.
Well, there's thirteen hundred and fifty-two guitar pickers
in Nashville
And they can pick more notes than the number of ants on
a Tennessee ant hill
Yeah, there's thirteen hundred and fifty-two guitar cases
in Nashville
And anyone of them packs his guitar could play twice as
better than I will
Yes, I was just 13, you might say I was a musical per-
verbial knee-high
When I heard a couple new soundin' tunes on the tubes
and they blasted me sky high
And the record man said everyone is a yellow sun record
from Nashville
And up north here ain't nobody buys 'em
And I said but I will and it was
Nashville cats
Play clean as country water
Nashville cats
Play wild as mountain dew
Nashville cats
Been playin' since they'se babies
Nashville cats
It worked before that too.

© Copyright 1966 by Faithful Virtue Music Co., Inc. Used by permission. All rights reserved.

Well, there's 16 thousand 800 and 21 mothers from Nashville
All their friends play music and they ain't up tight if one of the kids will
Because it's custom-made for any mother's son to be a guitar picker in Nashville and I sure am glad I got a chance to say a word about the music and the mothers from Nashville
Nashville cats
Play clean as country water
Nashville cats
Play wild as mountain dew
Nashville cats
Been playin' since they'se babies
Nashville cats
It worked before that too.

Jerry Reed

Guitar Man

Well, I quit my job down at the car wash
I left my momma a goodbye note
By sundown I'd left Kingston
With my guitar under my coat
I hitchhiked all the way down to Memphis
Got a room at the YMCA
For the next three weeks I went a-huntin' in nightclubs
Looking for a place to play
Well, I thought my pickin' would set 'em on fire
But nobody wanted to hire a guitar man.

Well, I nearly 'bout starved to death down in Memphis
I run out of money and luck
So I bought me a ride down to Macon, Ga., on an overloaded poultry truck
I thought of goin' down to Panama City
Started pickin' out some of them all-night bars
Hopin' I could make myself a dollar makin' music on my guitar
I got the same old story at them all-night peers
There ain't no room around here for a guitar man
(We don't need a guitar man, son).

So I slept in the hobo jungles
Roamed a thousand miles of track
Till I found myself at Mobile, Alabama at a club they call Big Jacks
A little four-piece band was jamming
So I took my guitar and I sat in
I showed 'em what a band would sound like with a swinging little guitar man
(Show 'em son).

© Copyright 1967 by Vector Music Corp.

If you ever take a trip down to the ocean
Find yourself down around Mobile
Make it on out to a club called Jacks
If you got a little time to kill
Just follow that crowd of people
You'll wind up out on his dance floor
Diggin' the finest little five-piece group
Up and down they come from Mexico
Guess who's leading that five-piece band
Wouldn't you know it's that swinging little guitar man,
yeah, yeah.

PART TEN

I used to live in New York City
Everything there was dark and dirty
Outside my window was a steeple
With a clock that always said twelve thirty

—JOHN PHILLIPS

Gerry Goffin/Carole King

Up on the Roof

When this old world starts getting me down
And people are just too much for me to face
I climb way up to the top of the stairs
And all my cares just drift right into space
On the roof it's peaceful as can be
And there the world below can't bother me
Let me tell you now
I don't melt in the sweltering heat
I go up where the air is fresh and sweet
I get away from the hustling crowds
And all that rat race noise down in the street
On the roof's the only place I know
Where you just have to wish to make it so
Up on the roof
At night the stars put on a show for free
And, darling, you can share it all with me
I keep a-tellin' you
Right smack dab in the middle of town
I found a Paradise that's trouble-proof
And if this world starts getting you down
There's room enough for two up on the roof.

© Copyright 1962 by Screen Gems–Columbia Music, Inc., New York, N.Y. Used by permission. Reproduction prohibited.

Barry Mann/Cynthia Weil/Jerry Leiber/ Mike Stoller

On Broadway

I hear the neon lights are bright
On Broadway
I hear that dreams come true there every day
I hear that life don't get you down
The way it gets you in this old town
I swear I'm gonna get me there some day
They say the girls all dress so fine
On Broadway
They say there ain't a thing there you can't buy
They say that you can be someone
And it don't matter where you come from
I swear I've got to get there or I'll die.

© Copyright 1963, 1964 by Screen Gems–Columbia Music, Inc., New York, N.Y. Used by permission. Reproduction prohibited.

Artie Resnick/Kenny Young

Under the Boardwalk

When the sun beats down
And melts the tar up on the roof
And your shoes get so hot
You wish your tired feet
Were fireproof
Under the boardwalk, down by the sea
On a blanket with my baby's where I'll be
From the park you hear
The happy sound of a carousel
And you can almost taste
The hot dogs and french fries they sell
Under the boardwalk, down by the sea
On a blanket with my baby's where I'll be
Under the boardwalk, out of the sun
Under the boardwalk, havin' some fun
Under the boardwalk, people walkin' above
Under the boardwalk, we'll be makin' love
Under the boardwalk.

© 1964 T. M. Music, Inc. Used by permission. All rights reserved.

John Phillips

California Dreamin'

All the leaves are brown,
And the sky is gray
I've been for a walk on a winter's day
I'd be safe and warm if I was in L.A.
California dreamin' on such a winter's day
Stopped into a church,
I passed along the way
I got down on my knees, and pretended to pray
You know the preacher likes the cold
He knows I'm going to stay
California dreamin' on such a winter's day.
If I didn't tell her I could leave today
California dreamin' on such a winter's day.
All the leaves are brown,
And the sky is gray
I've been for a walk on a winter's day
I'd be safe and warm if I was in L.A.
California dreamin' on such a winter's day.

© Copyright 1965 Wingate Music Corp., 1330 Avenue of the Americas, New York, N.Y. 10019. All rights reserved. Used by permission.

John Sebastian/Mark Sebastian/Steve Boone

Summer in the City

Hot town, summer in the city
Back o' my neck gettin' dirt and gritty
Been down, isn't it a pity
Doesn't seem to be a shadow in the city
All around, people lookin' half dead
Walkin' on the sidewalk,
Hotter than a match head
But tonight it's a different world
Go out and find a girl
Come on, come on and dance all night
Despite the heat it'll be all right
And babe, don't you know it's a pity
The days can't be like the nights
In the summer in the city
In the summer in the city
Cool town, evening in the city
Dressed so fine and lookin' so pretty
Cool cat, lookin' for a kitty
Gonna look in every corner of the city
Till I'm wheezing like a bus stop
Runnin' up the stairs
Gonna meet you on the rooftop
Come on, come on and dance all night
Despite the heat it'll be all right
And babe, don't you know it's a pity
The days can't be like the nights
In the summer in the city.

© Copyright 1966 by Faithful Virtue Music Co., Inc. Used by permission. All rights reserved.

John Phillips

Twelve Thirty (Young Girls Are Coming to the Canyon)

I used to live in New York City
Everything there was dark and dirty
Outside my window was a steeple
With a clock that always said twelve thirty.

Young girls are coming to the canyon
And in the mornings I can see them walking
I can no longer keep my blinds drawn
And I can't keep myself from talking.

At first so strange to feel so friendly
To say good morning and really mean it
To feel these changes happening in me
But not to notice till I feel it.
(Repeat chorus).

Cloudy waters cast no reflection
Images of beauty lie there stagnant
Vibrations bounce in no direction
And lie there shattering into fragments.
(Repeat chorus).

© Copyright 1967 Wingate Music Corp., 1330 Avenue of the Americas, New York, N.Y. 10019. All rights reserved. Used by permission.

Joe McDonald

Harlem Song

Glorious . . . breathtaking . . . spectacular!
Relax in the grandeur of America's yesteryear
Harlem—land of enchanting contrasts,
Where the romantic past touches hands
With the exciting present
First, the pleasure of being received
With warmth and genuine hospitality
Then, the easy adjustment to the comfort and style
Of superb meals, exotic beverages, colorful entertainment
And dynamite action
Doing all the wonderful things
That wonderful vacations are made of
At wonderful savings, too.
Yes, come to Harlem
The happy meeting ground for families with large wants
And small budgets . . .

See colorful Harlem in New York City
Come treat yourself to some grits and barbecue
Bring the family to Harlem in New York City
For a summer of fun dancing to the rhythm and blues—
And if you're looking for the action, this summer is your chance
All the black folks are just dying to watch you sing and dance
In colorful Harlem, that's New York City
Where every soulful spade has a serenade just for you . . .

"Well, hi, baby how you doin' today?"
"Howdy do, man, I ain't feelin' so good, you know?"

Copyright © 1968 Joyful Wisdom. Used by permission.

"What's the matter, baby?"

"Well, I was sitting around the house, you know, and me and the old lady was sitting down ready to have a good meal of watermelon and hominy grits, we all set, and they's showin' a whole bunch of reruns of the Amos 'n' Andy Show, you know?"

"My favorite program!"

"Yeah, well, the TV blew out right in the middle of the program, man!"

"Well, what'd you do then?"

"What does it look like I did? I came outside and ran into you—jerk!"

"Well . . . I'll tell you—everything's blowin' up these days—TV's, ghettos, you know, it's getting kinda rough."

"Yeah. They even made a movie out of it."

"What'd they call it?"

"Blow-up!"

"Pretty funny!"

"Well, it looks like I'll be shufflin' off now, you know?"

"Yeah, well, with all that natural rhythm you can probably shuffle pretty good . . ."

Discover glorious Harlem in New York City
There's thrills and chills in the land of rhythm and blues
Bring the family to Harlem in New York City
They'll have fun in the sun doin' what the black folks do
And every little pickaninny
Wears a great big grin
Just hanging round and waiting
For some white folks to drop in
But if you can't go to Harlem—that's New York City
Maybe you'll be lucky and Harlem will come to you . . . .

PART ELEVEN

You know I couldn't get high
And I don't know why

—KEN WEAVER

Jerry Leiber/Mike Stoller

Love Potion #9

I took my troubles down to Madam Ruth
You know, that gypsy with the gold-capped tooth
She's got a pad down at 34th and Vine
Sellin' little bottles of Love Potion #9
I told her that I was a flop with chicks
"I've been this way since 1956"
She looked at my palm and she made a magic sign
She said, "What you need is Love Potion #9"
She bent and turned around and gave me a wink
She said, "I'm gonna mix it up right here in the sink"
It smelled like turpentine and looked like India ink
I held my nose, I closed my eyes, I took a drink
I didn't know if it was day or night
I started kissing everything in sight
But when I kissed the cop down at 34th and Vine
He broke my little bottle of Love Potion #9
I had so much fun that I'm goin' back again—
I wonder what happens with Love Potion #10?

© 1959 Quintet Music. Used by permission.

Tandyn Almer

Along Comes Mary

Everytime I think that I'm the only one who's lonely
Someone calls on me
And every now and then, I spend my time at rhyme and
verse
And curse the faults in me
But then, along comes Mary
And does she wanna give me kicks
And be my steady chick and give me
Pick of memories?
Or maybe rather gather tales
From all the fails and tribulations
No one ever sees?

When we met
I was out to lunch
Now my empty cup tastes
As sweet as the punch.

When vague desire is the fire in the eyes of chicks
Whose sickness is the games they play
And when the masquerade is played and neighbor folks
Make jokes at who is most to blame today
Then along comes Mary
And does she wanna set them free
And make them see the realities in which
She got her name?
And will they struggle much when told that such
A tender touch of hers will make them
Not the same?

When we met
I was sure out to lunch

© Copyright 1965, 1967 Irving Music, Inc. Used by permission.

Now my empty cup tastes
As sweet as the punch.

Then when the morning of the warning's passed,
The gassed and flaccid kids are flung across the stars
The psychodramas and the traumas gone, the songs are left unsung
And hung upon the scars
And then along comes Mary
And does she wanna see the stains
The dead remains of all the pains
She sent the night before?
Or will their waking eyes reflect the lies
And realize their urgent cry
For sight no more?

When we met
I was sure out to lunch
Now my empty cup tastes
As sweet as the punch.

Ken Weaver

I Couldn't Get High

I went to a party the other night
I wanted to fill my brain with light
So I grabbed me a bottle and I started drinkin' wine
I thought pretty soon I'd be feelin' fine

But I couldn't get high
And I don't know why

So I threw down the bottle
And I whipped out my pipe
I stuffed it full of grass
And I gave it a light
I huffed and I puffed
And I smoked and I toqued
But after a while
My heart was nearly broke

'Cause I couldn't get high
And I don't know why

So I threw down my pipe
As mad as I could be
And I gobbled up a cube
Of LSD
So I waited thirty minutes
For my body to sing
Yeah, I waited and waited
But I couldn't feel a thing

You know I couldn't get high
And I don't know why

© 1965 Heavy Metal Music, Inc.

As hard as I tried
I couldn't get high
I couldn't get high.

Gene Clark/David Crosby/Jim McGuinn

Eight Miles High

Eight miles high,
And when you touch down
You'll find that
It's stranger than known.

Signs in the street
That say where you're going
Are somewhere just
Being their own.

Nowhere is
Their warmth to be found
Among those afraid
Of losing their ground.

Rain, gray town
Known for its sound
In places
Small faces unbound.

Round the squares
Huddled in storms
Some laughing
Some just shapeless forms.

Sidewalk scenes,
And black limousines.
Some living
Some standing alone.

© 1966 Tickson Music Co.

Jim McGuinn

5-D

Oh, how is it that I'd come out to here
And still be floating
And never hit bottom but keep falling through
Just relaxed and paying attention?
All my two-dimensional boundaries were gone
I had lost them badly
I saw that world crumble and thought I was dead
But I found my senses still working
And as I continued to drop through the hole
I found all surroundings to show me
That joy innocently is
Just be quiet and feel it all around you
And I opened my heart to the whole universe
And I found it was loving
And I saw the great blunder my teachers had made
Scientific delirium madness
O—
I will keep falling as long as I live
Or without ending
I will remember the place that is now
That has ended before the beginning
O how is it that I'd come out to here
And still be floating
And never hit bottom but keep falling through
Just relaxed and paying attention?

© 1966 Tickson Music Co.

Frank Zappa

Are You Hung Up?

ARE YOU HUNG UP?
ARE YOU HUNG UP?
ARE YOU HUNG UP?
ARE YOU HUNG UP?
ARE YOU HUNG UP?
ARE YOU HUNG UP?
Who needs the Peace Corps?
What's there to live for?
Who needs the Peace Corps?
Think I'll just DROP OUT
I'll go to Frisco
Buy a wig and sleep on Owsley's floor
Walk past the wig store
Dance at the Fillmore
I'm completely stoned
I'm hippy and I'm trippy
I'm a gypsy on my own
I'll stay a week and get the crabs
And take a bus back home
I'm really just a phony
But forgive me 'cause I'm stoned
Every town must have a place
Where phony hippies meet
Psychedelic dungeons popping up on every street
GO TO SAN FRANCISCO. . . .

© 1968 by Frank Zappa Music, Inc. All rights reserved.

PART TWELVE

I wanna go home, I wanna go home,
oh lord I wanna go home

—DANNY DILL/MEL TILLIS

John Loudermilk

Tobacco Road

I was born in a dump
Mama died and daddy got drunk
Left me here to die or grow
In the middle of Tobacco Road
Grew up in a rusty shack
All I owned was a-hangin' on my back
Only Lord knows how I loathe
The place called Tobacco Road
But it's home, the only life I ever knowed
But the Lord knows I loathe Tobacco Road
But I loves you 'cause you're home
Gonna leave, get a job
With the help and the grace of God
Save my money, get rich I know
Bring it back to Tobacco Road
Bring dynamite and a crane
Blow it up and start over again
Build a town, be proud to show
Keep the name of Tobacco Road
'Cause it's the only life I knowed
I despise you 'cause you're filthy
Tobacco Road
But I loves you 'cause you're home.

© 1960 Cedarwood Publishing Co., Inc.

Danny Dill/Mel Tillis

Detroit City

Last night I went to sleep in Detroit City
And I dreamed about the cotton fields and home
I dreamed about my mother, dear old papa, sister and
 brother
And I dreamed about the girl who's been waiting for so
 long
I wanna go home, I wanna go home, I wanna go home,
 oh lord I wanna go home.

Home folks think I'm big in Detroit City
From the letters that I write they think I'm fine
But by day I make the cars
By night I make the bars
If only they could read between the lines
I wanna go home, I wanna go home, oh lord I wanna go
 home.

'Cause you know I rode a freight train
North to Detroit City
And after all these years
I find I've just been wasting my time.

So I just think I'll take my foolish pride
And put it on the south-bound freight and ride
And go on back to the loved ones
The ones that I left waiting so far behind.

© 1962 Cedarwood Publishing Co., Inc.

Randy Newman

So Long, Dad

Home again
And the streets are not much cleaner
And the quaint old south side scenery
Is quaint no more
Just older than before
Up the stairs and down the hallway
To my daddy's door
"Your son is home, dad, and he's found a girl
Well, she's the greatest girl in all the world
I think you'll like her, dad, I hope you do
And if you don't that's all right too.
What's new?
Do you still work at the drugstore?
Is that true?
Still polishing the same floor?"
Miss my good old dad!
"My, but I'm glad to see you
Home again, but we won't be staying here, dad
Come and see us, papa, when you can
There'll always be a place for my old man
Just drop by when it's convenient to
Be sure to call before you do—
So long, now."

© 1967 January Music Corporation, a subsidiary of A. Schroeder Music Corporation. All rights reserved. International copyright secured.

Steve Cropper/Otis Redding

(Sittin' on) The Dock of the Bay

Sittin' in the morning sun
I'll be sittin' when the evening comes
Watching the ships roll in
Then I watch 'em roll away again, yeah
I'm sittin' on the dock of the bay
Watching that tide roll in
Just sittin' on the dock of the bay
wastin' time.

I left my home in Georgia
Headed for the Frisco Bay
I had nothing to live for
Looks like nothing's gonna come my way
So I'm just sittin' on the dock of the bay
Watching the tide roll in
I'm sittin' on the dock of the bay
wastin' time.

Looks like nothing's gonna change
Everything still remains the same
I can't do what ten people tell me to do
So I guess I'll remain the same
Just sittin' here resting my bones
And this loneliness won't leave me alone
This 2,000 miles I roamed just to make this dock my home
Now I'm sittin' on the dock of the bay
Watching the tide roll in
Sittin' on the dock of the bay
wastin' time.

© 1968 East/Memphis Music Corp., Time Music Co., Inc., and Redwal Music Co., Inc. Reprinted by permission of the publishers.

THIS PAGE IS DEDICATED TO
BOB DYLAN,
WHOSE LYRICS, REGRETTABLY,
WERE UNAVAILABLE AT PRESS TIME.

There is one—and only one—
authorized biography of the Beatles.
This nationwide bestseller is it!

The Beatles

by Hunter Davies

Not too many years ago, Ringo, Paul, John, and George were middle-class English schoolboys. Today, they're the Beatles. Millionaires. Celebrities. And outrageously controversial.

Here is their complete and unexpurgated story, written by a man who traveled with the famous group for sixteen months. It is the story of four very intelligent, very talented, and very human young men caught in the act of symbolizing our era. Even people who have managed to resist their charm will find THE BEATLES a fascinating book. Illustrated.

A DELL BOOK 95¢

If you cannot obtain copies of this title at your local bookseller, just send the price (plus 10c per copy for handling and postage) to Dell Books, Box 2291, Grand Central Post Office, New York, N.Y. 10017. No postage or handling charge is required on any order of five or more books.